MOM

MOM

A Pocket Treasure Book for a Dear Mom

Andrews McMeel Publishing

Kansas City

Mom: A Pocket Treasure Book for a Dear Mom
Copyright © 2006 by River House Media, Inc.
All rights reserved. Printed in China.
No part of this book may be used or reproduced
in any manner whatsoever without written permission,
except in the case of reprints in the context of reviews.
For information write Andrews McMeel Publishing,
an Andrews McMeel Universal company,
4520 Main Street, Kansas City, Missouri 64111.

06 07 08 09 10 EPB 10 9 8 7 6 5 4 3 2 1

ISBN-13: 978-0-7407-5840-9
ISBN-10: 0-7407-5840-3

www.andrewsmcmeel.com

POCKET TREASURES™ is a trademark of
River House Media, Inc.
POCKET TREASURES™ are produced by Jean Lowe,
River House Media, Inc., Leawood, Kansas

Design by Delsie Chambon

I couldn't *wish* for a better mom...

one who
loves me on my
good days

and my **bad**,

at my **best**
and at my
worst,

and still *loves* me,

all of me,

just the way

I am.

One that has all the **tricks** up her sleeve, all the *magic* in her wand—

and all
the love
in her *heart*
to fix any and all
of my ills ...

whether they
be tears of
sorrow,

or a **fever** and
the **chills.**

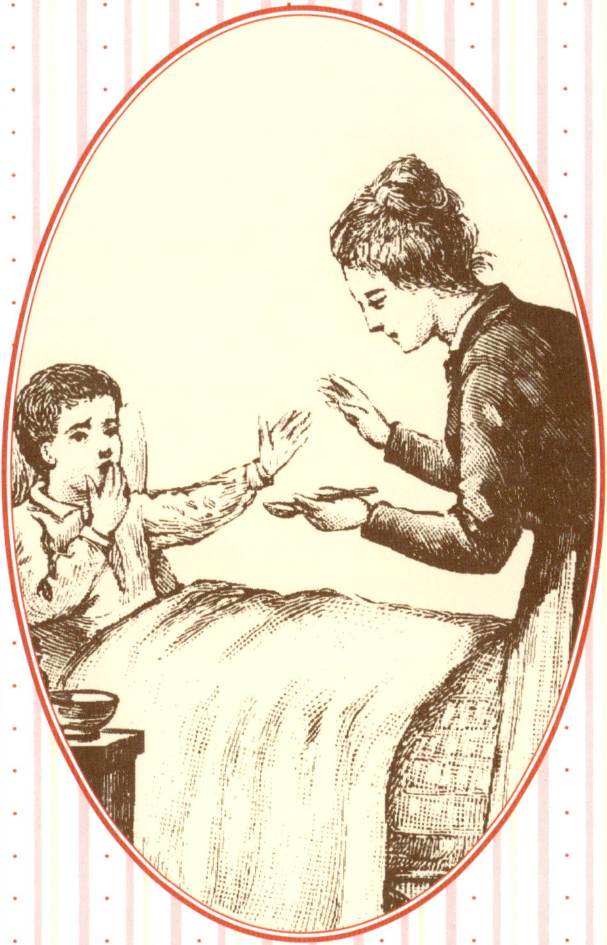

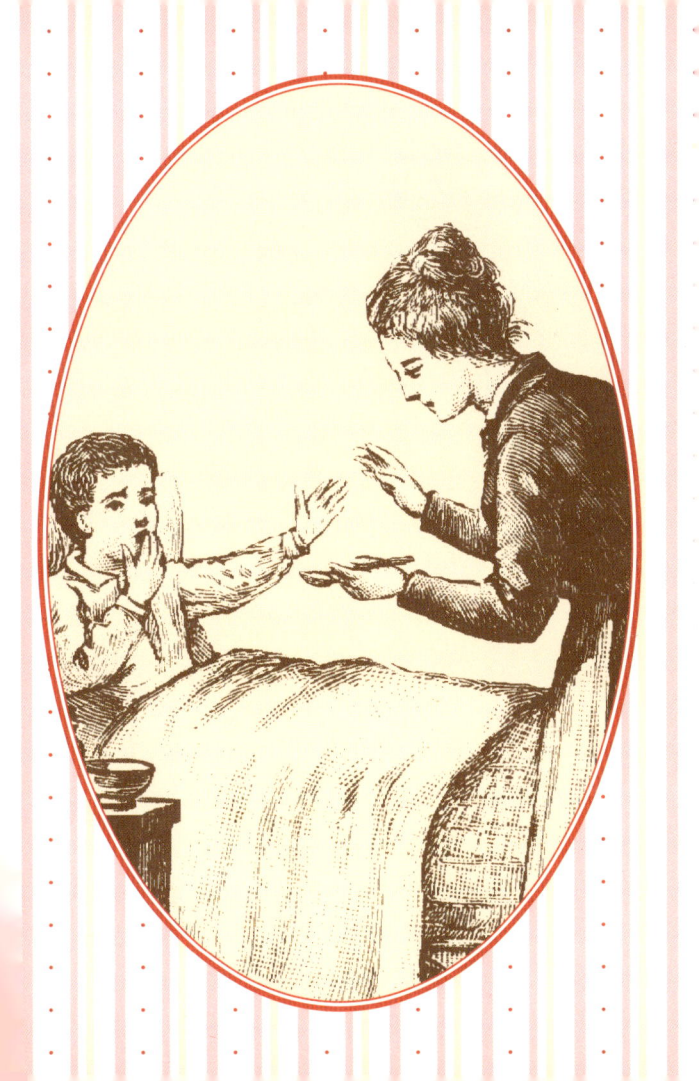

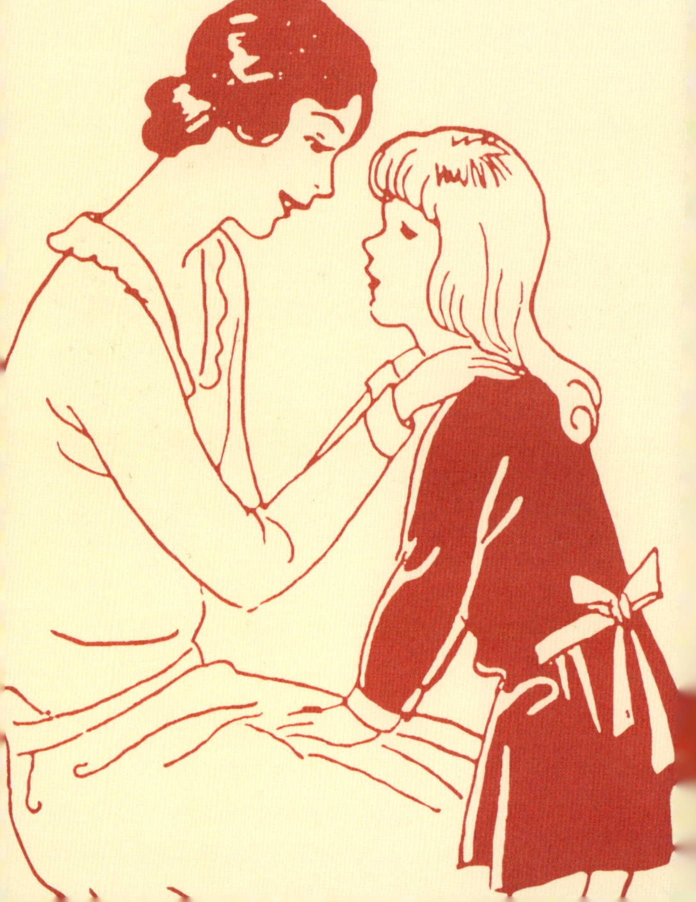

Sometimes, she's the only one *loving* enough to tell me like it *really* is.

Because she is more than my **mom**—

she's my *friend.*

I couldn't *wish* for a better mom..

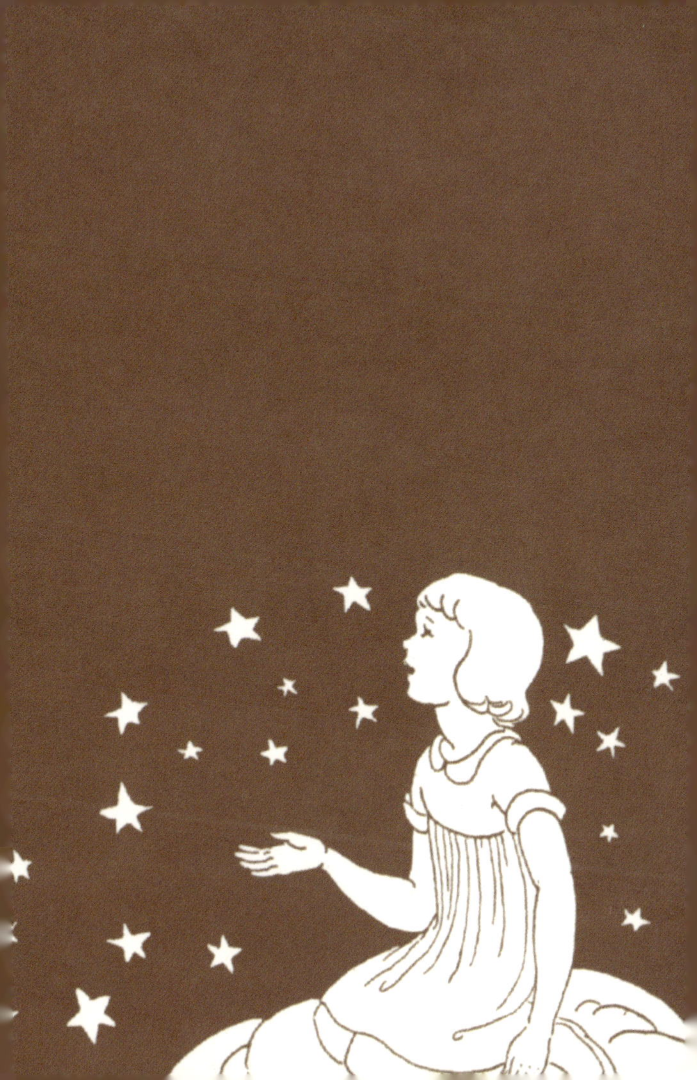

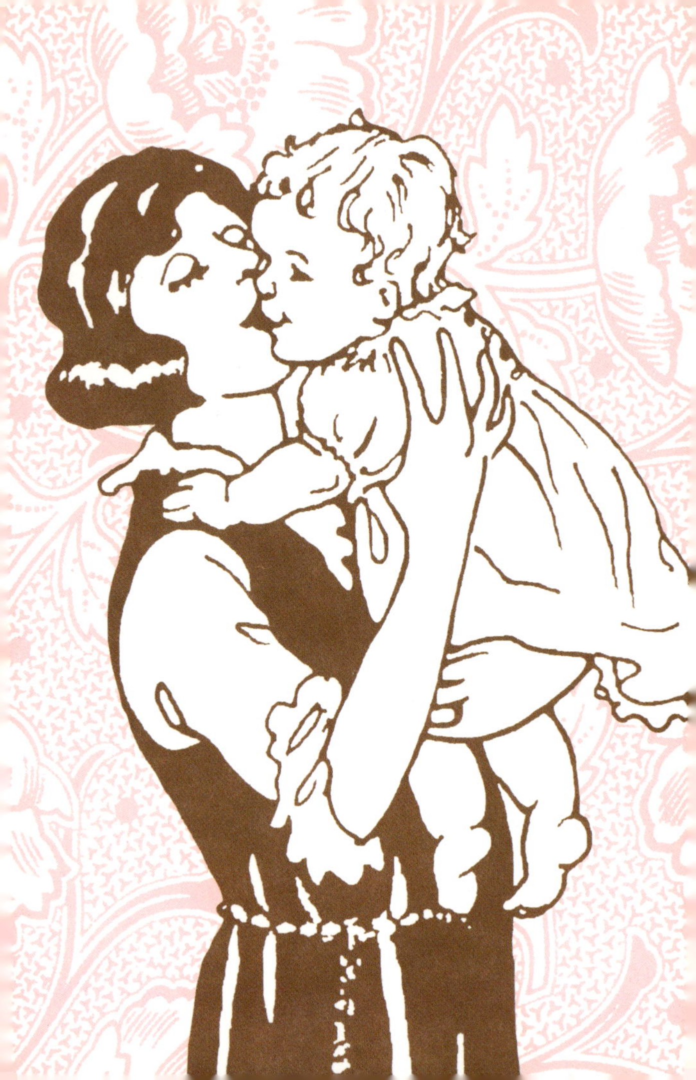

one who
understands
that *love*
is all it takes—

to bring out
the **best**
in someone.

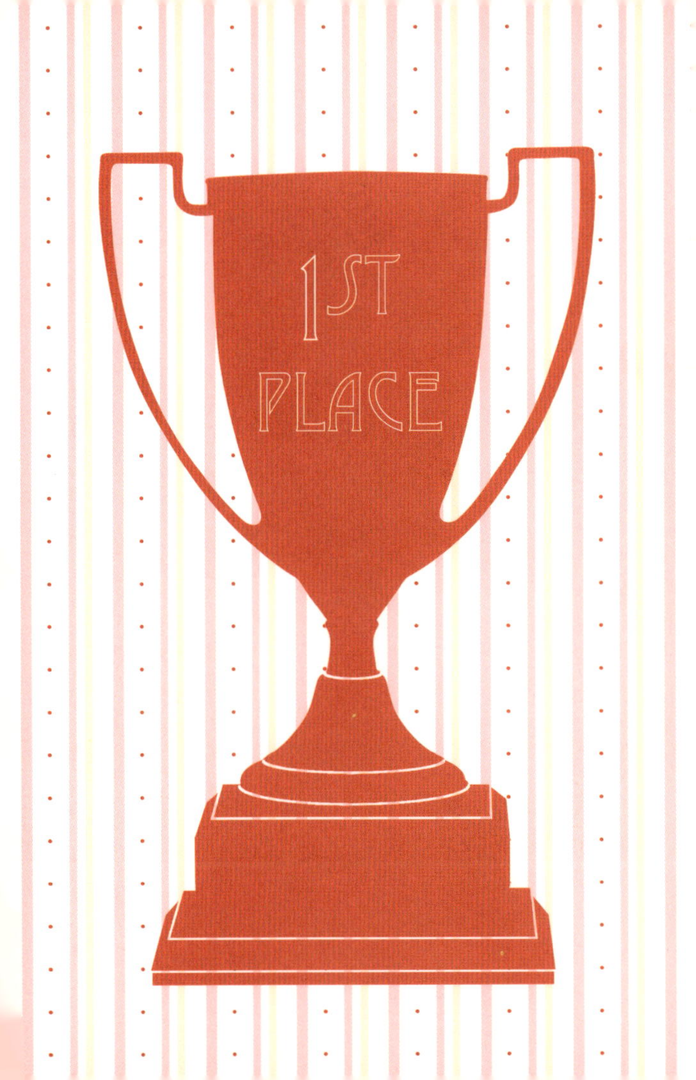
1ST
PLACE

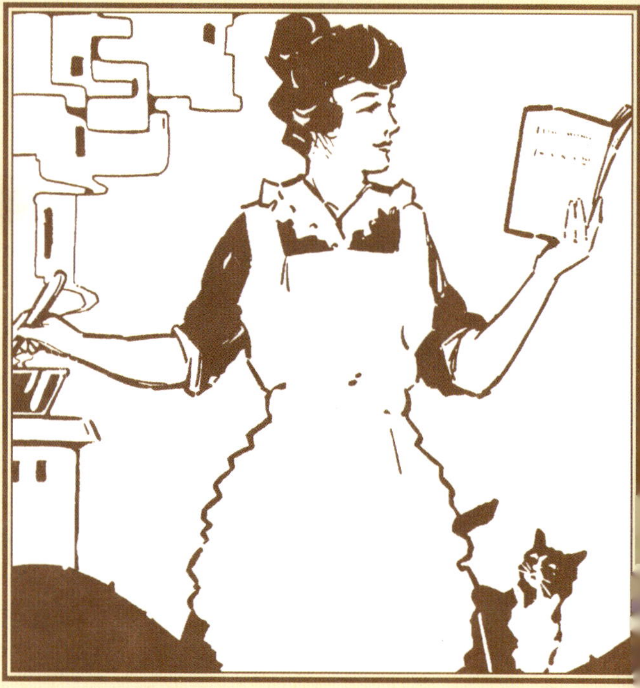

And that **hugs** and home-cooked meals never go out of style.

One who
continues
to bring out

the
best
in me...

and that
includes my

smile!

Mom,
I'm so happy
to be yours!
And you
are mine...